Echoes of the Spirit

Women's Prayers and Meditations

Compiled and Edited by
Margaret Graham Beers

Preface

For many of us praying is a solitary activity involving one person, alone, communicating with God. If praying is personal, idiosyncratic to each individual, of what use are other people's prayers?

What use? The impulse to be connected to fellow human beings is strong in each person. In prayer, the sense of a common purpose, a common situation of helplessness and powerlessness in relationship to God, underscores our connection to each other, as we seek to know and to be known by God.

Prayers are like jumper-cables; they re-start conversation with God and help us feel the connection that is always available. Prayers connect

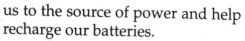

us to the source of power and help recharge our batteries.

People have been composing prayers since the dawn of time—prayers that help to develop a relationship with God and share that relationship with others. At the end of the Twentieth Century avenues for spiritual expression are much broader for women than heretofore. Thus, this collection contains contributions from women clergy—a blessed dividend of their admission into ordained ministry—which have a special corporate sensibility beyond the personal quality of the lay writers.

The prayers gathered here exhibit a richness unique to the church today and to our lives as men and women under God.

—Peggy Beers
Editor

Holy Women

Guide us by your love, Jesus.

Our feet to follow your way,
   as the women who traveled
   with you.

Our hands to offer kindness,
   as the woman who anointed
   you with oil.

Our hearts to stay despite fear,
   as the women at the foot of
   the Cross.

Our eyes to the empty tomb,
   as the women who came on
   the third day.

Our ears to hear and know you,
   as Mary's when you spoke
   her name.

Our mouths to tell of you to all,
   as the women who told you
   had risen.

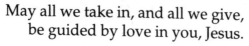

May all we take in, and all we give,
be guided by love in you, Jesus.

Amen.

—Wendy Abrahamson

We Live

We live
   in the circle of life.
We live
   in the embrace of love.
We live
   in the unending blessing of
   salvation.
We live
   in the love of God. *Amen.*

—Vienna Cobb Anderson

Morning

I arise
    in the blessing of God's love.

I arise
    in the hope of a day of
    fulfillment:
        in the meaning of life,
        in the challenges of work,
        in the wonder of play,
        in the joy of relationship.

I arise
    in the joyful certainty of being
    loved:
        Christ before me,
        Christ beside me,
        Christ behind me,
        Christ ever with me.

I arise
    in the wonder and beauty of
    God's creation:
        the sun to delight,

the rain to bless,
the clouds to stir
    imagination,
the winds to cool,
the flowers to offer smiles,
the waters in which to frolic,
the birds, animals and
    insects to give
    companionship,
the earth to nurture my
    body and soul.

I arise
    stepping forth
        In the blessing of God's Love.
            Amen.

—Vienna Cobb Anderson

Suburban Litany

O God, we have meant to love and serve you better than we do, but we have not. Our streets are lined with trees, our houses warm, our friends good, our children well-fed. We have meant to thank you with our lives, but we have not.

> *O God, forgive us and*
> *teach us your ways.*

We have meant to listen to your voice, but we have been too busy to hear you very often. When we have heard you, we have meant to obey you, but we have forgotten, or at times we have been too afraid.

> *O God, forgive us and*
> *teach us your ways.*

We have set up a comfortable family life as our highest goal and closed our eyes to the greater demands of your love. We have filled our lives with too many things to do and too many things to care for.

> *O God, forgive us and*
> *teach us your ways.*

We have set ourselves apart from our poorer city neighbors, and sometimes we forget that they are even there. We try not to think of the hungry in other lands too often because there are so many.

> *O God, forgive us and*
> *teach us your ways.*

We have lived in anxiety lest our private world explode in pain and terror, and we have looked towards fear and away from you.

> *O God, forgive us and*
> *teach us your ways.*

We have meant to serve you in everything we do, but we have given you only the leftover hour, the spare energy and the momentary prayer.

> *O God, forgive us and
> teach us your ways.*

Amen.

—Avery Brooke
(with permission[1])

Holy Presence

My Lord and my God,

How can I understand the depths
   of your creation?

If I go to green tall trees, mountains
   and meadows—

> *You are there.*

If I go to arid, dry, dusty plateaus—

> *You are there.*

If I go to hot and humid tropical
   forests—

> *You are there.*

If I go to places of oppression and
   deprivation—

> *You are there.*

If I go to places of wealth and
   privilege—

You are there.

If I go to places of misunderstanding, confusion and hostility—

You are there.

If I go to the places where I feel sad and guilty—

You are there.

If I go to where the sick and dying live with hopelessness and hopefulness—all at once— yearning for you—

You are there.

And even when I go into the dark night of my soul—

You are there.

I love you and thank you!

Amen.

—Patti Browning

Forgiveness

Dearest Jesus,

You have lived a life of such incredible, overwhelming affirmation, and incredible, overwhelming rejection. How can such a contradiction be justified or named? You taught me through all of the unjust sufferings that you endured, what true forgiveness really means.

But this can never mean that I will ever be totally forgiving or totally loving as you are. I can only hold you up as my goal that I shall never reach—my role model and my savior. Please help me, dearest Lord, to love all of your creation; help me to reach out to those who see you differently from me, and help me to bridge the gap.

Thank you for loving *all* of us.

Amen.

—Patti Browning

A Portable Prayer

When I was diagnosed with stage three breast cancer, I was scared. I searched for prayers that reflected my fear, sadness, aloneness as I experienced a lumpectomy and three months of chemotherapy. I found some good prayers that were too long to memorize. On Epiphany, I was in a Roman Catholic hospital for a mastectomy. Crucifixes looked down at me in every room. As I lay awake at night, Jesus' presence was palpable. I found myself talking to Jesus as if he were there. He understood. A mantra came to me that helped me breathe deeply and relax while concentrating on Jesus—with me, not on the cross. I prayed for the things I needed:

Come, Jesus, come.
Hold my hand.

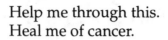

Help me through this.
Heal me of cancer.

Over the weeks, this evolved into
a meditation during chemotherapy
and radiation. Lying absolutely
still for ten to fifteen minutes in an
uncomfortable position, I would
picture Jesus as a Star Trek hero,
aiming the rays where needed
most and guiding the therapist.
When I am hurt or fearful, Jesus
holds me. A gentle person has
helped me through this and will
heal me.

Come, Jesus, come.
Hold me
Help me.
Heal me. *Amen.*

—Sally Bucklee

Bless the Light

Bless the winter light glazing the
    frozen surface of the pond
    pink;

Bless the spring light trickling
    through
silky green leaves, one shimmer-
    ing drop at a time;

Bless the summer light slipping
    slowly down
blue mountains thick as golden
    syrup;

Bless the autumn light igniting
    streams
and fields, flaming red and ochre
    and gold;

Bless the light, bless the Lord,
Bless this luminous life. *Amen.*

—Emily Chewning

A Prayer for Discernment

Lord, I am listening, and I can't
    hear anything
but the noise my heart is making.
What is it You have for my life?

Where are You?

I keep going over and over the
    same ground,
and I don't find you there.

I surrender and walk out
into this new spring morning.
Overnight, wild violets sprouted
    in the grass,
one white lilac is blooming
    on the bush,
billows of bluebells hug
    the stone wall,
a breeze carries the scent of
    lavender and mint.

Lord, You are here.

Forgive my impatience.
Forgive my doubt.

Gracious God,
you feed me with a vision
of wonder
of the infinite possibilities
of the beauty of your plan
for creation.

You quiet my heart with hope,
and I am reminded of your
promise.

Expect joy in the morning.

In Your time, not mine,
I pray for discernment. *Amen.*

—Emily Chewning

For the General Convention

We thank you, O God, for all you give us in the abundance of your creation. Especially, we pray that you will give to the General Convention the presence of your Holy Spirit that we may govern ourselves according to your will. May your spirit so guide us that when we are confused you will give us wisdom. When we are lost, give us direction. When we are divided, give us openness. When we are tired, give us perseverance. When we take ourselves too seriously, give us humor. Under your guidance and love may we emerge from these deliberations faithful stewards committed to the unity of the church and its mission to the troubled world, so that all our actions may be to the glory of your name and the furthering of your Spirit; in the name of your Son, Jesus Christ, who gave to us the command to love one another.

Amen.

—Pamela P. Chinnis

For Families Stricken by Strife

In the innocence of every child we glimpse what you intend for us. In the faces of the very old, we see a treasury of wisdom for the human family, the stories and traditions that nourish and instruct. In the love of mothers and fathers we see your love that gives its life for the beloved. Allow protection for the vulnerable to fall gently upon the very young and very old in strife-torn countries that they may be preserved from violence and danger. Give to the parents the ability to carry out the sacred trust of raising their children in places of safety and peace. Give those charged with helping those at the dawn and dusk of life such aid as is best for them and restore them speedily to homes of quiet and dignity. *Amen.*

—Barbara Crafton

Getting Free

How can I help others
When I am not Free?
What is Free?
Free is spaciousness,
        unboundedness,
Going with the flow, airborne.
Free is fluid, unconstrained,

Loose, liquid, malleable.
Art is Free: colorful, rhythmic.
Art is life—filling all the spaces.
Life. Art. Freedom.
God gives me Freedom
He has mounted me with wings
   like eagles. *Amen.*

—Elizabeth Cook

For the Homeless

We pray this day for the walking
wounded who live without shelter
and food. Their lives are confused,
their minds scattered, their insecu-
rities and fears abundant. They
live on city streets, under bridges,
in boxes and plastic tenting. They
sleep in parks, on church steps,
curled up in doorways. They are
the rejected of society, cast away
with no one to call them by name.

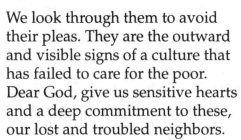

We look through them to avoid
their pleas. They are the outward
and visible signs of a culture that
has failed to care for the poor.
Dear God, give us sensitive hearts
and a deep commitment to these,
our lost and troubled neighbors.

Amen.

—Meg Graham

Enlarge My Heart

Dearest One:
Increase the capacity of my heart.
Take its edges and stretch them out
To include all in me that I do not
    love,
All in my family that I judge,
All in my church that I fear,
All in my world that doesn't fit.

Amen.

—Phoebe Griswold

Support

Jesus reach for me
Spirit strengthen me
God catch me.

—Phoebe Griswold

Exultation

Holy One, make me supple and
strong in your hands! *Amen.*

—Peggy Gunness

Desire

Oh Jesus
Capture my heart
once more.
Let it fly
with love for you.

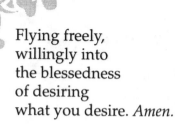

Flying freely,
willingly into
the blessedness
of desiring
what you desire. *Amen.*

—Betty Hedblom

Remembrance

Help us to remember, O God,
when your promises seem prepos-
terous, the laughter of our sister,
Sarah, who by your grace became
the mother of nations;

Help us to remember, when we
feel listless and dull, the exuber-
ance of our sister, Miriam, who
made music, dancing and singing,
rejoicing in God's mighty acts;

Help us to remember, when we
feel helpless against evil, the

ingenuity of our mid-wife sisters,
Shiphrah and Puah, who defied
Pharaoh's edict so that Hebrew
infants might live;

Help us to remember, when we
feel insignificant and unknown,
the prophecy of our sister Huldah,
greatly esteemed in her time but
barely visible in the annals of
sacred history;

Help us to remember, when we
feel bereft and forsaken, the
patient persistence of our sister
Hannah, whose long-barren womb
God blessed with a son;

Help us to remember, when we
feel self-important, the humility of
our sister Elizabeth, who knew
that another would give birth to
the Lord;

Help us to remember when we
feel perplexed about our future,

the courage of our sister Mary, who said, *Let it be to me, according to your will,* even as her heart was pierced by a sword;

Help us to remember, when we feel unrecognized, the unstinting devotion of our unnamed sister of whom Jesus said, *Wherever the Gospel is preached in the whole world, what she has done will be told in memory of her.*

Help us to remember, when we feel ignored or rebuffed, the tenacity of our outcast sister, the Syro-Phoenician woman, whose faith Jesus extolled as he healed her daughter;

Help us to remember, when we feel over-burdened with responsibility, the wisdom of our sister Mary of Bethany, who sat at the feet of Jesus and received his teaching;

Help us to remember, when we feel unfairly maligned, the faithful witness of our sister Mary Magdalene, wrongly recalled as a harlot, yet the first to see the Risen Lord and first to proclaim the good news of the Resurrection.

We thank you God for the lives of these women. Help us to honor their names and to make their stories our own. Give us the wisdom, the courage and the perseverance to serve you in our generation as they did in theirs, that our witness to your love and your mercy may be a beacon of light for those who will follow. We ask this in the name of your son, who was born of a woman and whose broken and bloodied body women lovingly prepared for burial. *Amen.*

—Martha Horne

The Communion of Saints

There is a word which precedes
    all words
There is a word which contains
    all words
There is a word which belongs
    to God
        which defines Christ
        which inhabits the Spirit

This is the word which was at the
    beginning

It is the word which made the
    world
It is the word that created all that is
It is the word that tells us who we
    are
It is the word of greatest power
It is the word which Jesus proclaims
It is the word which Jesus works
It is the word which means Good
    News

It is the word which means Release
It is the word which means
    Recovery
It is the word which means Freedom
It is the word which means Favor
It is the word which means Whole

Without this word there is no
    healing
Without this word there is no
    connection
Without this word there is no
    communion

This word is the meaning of the
    Communion of Saints
This word is the energy of all that
    we are
This word is our vocation
This word is our calling
This word is our name

Our communion is born in this word
Our prayer springs from it
Our deep desire lives in it
Our hope rests on it

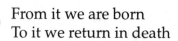

From it we are born
To it we return in death

This word says No to all that
    divides us
This word says No to all that is
    broken
This word says No to all that is ill
This word says No to all that is evil

This word says Yes to compassion
This word says Yes to connection
This word says Yes to communion

All the saints sing it
All the prophets proclaim it
All the martyrs die for it
All the children know it

The Communion of Saints lives in it
We live in it
It is our source and our destiny

The word is **one**

The Lord our God is **one**
All that is is **one** in God

We are **one** in God
We are **one**
The Communion of Saints is **one**

The Word is one. *Amen.*

—Anne Shelburne Jones

The Desert

The desert is where I am spiritually fed, fed by the faces of Bedouin children, fed by the blanket of stars that stud the night sky, fed by the presence of God in each living thing. I am a desert person. I believe we are a desert people and our faith comes out of the desert.

I go to the desert to see me. I go to find who is in charge of the way I live—me or the world or God. When I am in the desert I don't put on make-up, and I don't take a

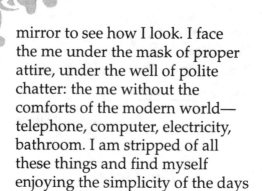

mirror to see how I look. I face
the me under the mask of proper
attire, under the well of polite
chatter: the me without the
comforts of the modern world—
telephone, computer, electricity,
bathroom. I am stripped of all
these things and find myself
enjoying the simplicity of the days
and nights. The desert strips me of
pretense, and I encounter the
person beyond all these things.

In the desert I meet Moses and
trek for two days where he and his
people trekked for forty years.
Like them, I murmur. I come to
know Elijah who yearned to hear
God's voice, and I share his
yearning. I burn with the passion
of God's love and am not
consumed. I stand on holy ground.

Within minutes of making camp,
the eyes and ears of the Sinai

appear in the form of Bedouin children. I stand among them. We laugh—the universal language. They sell their wares. Their nomadic lifestyle calls me to live more simply, to love more deeply, to seek God in every encounter. Their faces are the face of God. In those children, in the rugged rock, in the blanket of stars, in the oasis— that is where I see God—that is where I hear the still small voice.

The desert is the dry place where my faith begins, the place where I meet God. When all the trappings are stripped away, and I am no longer hiding behind the many faces I use, then I am able to see God, present and waiting and loving.

God is the gift the desert gives me.
Amen.

—Mary Page Jones

Seminary Baccalaureate

Most gracious God, you have
brought us to this day, and we
rejoice in it. We thank you for our
many blessings:

for life,
for your love for us,
for our new life in the resurrected
    Christ,
for the privilege of study,
for the efforts of others who have
    sustained us,
for our life together.

Through one another—in worship,
in debate, in conflict, in unity—we
have known anger and love more
fully. In our struggle to live in
community as the people of God
you have confronted us. We con-
fess our frailty and our sin.
Forgive us, heal us, renew us.

You have called and equipped us to minister in your name. Now we leave this place to spread the Gospel to the ends of the earth, as you command. The thought overwhelms us, as it overwhelmed the first disciples, but we know the Holy Spirit empowered them and will empower us.

So, we come to this day and pray that you will give us all we need to minister in your name and continue your work of redemption so that we may live as people born anew. Make us people of vision and courage. Teach us to order our lives according to your will. Make us people of discipline in an often chaotic world. May we go forth as people who speak and live the Gospel.

Lead us into communities where we may work for liberation. May

we work together with all people
against the forces of evil and
injustice.

Yes, God, we are indeed overwhelmed. We stand together with
the first disciples and tremble.
Come, Holy Spirit, anoint us for
this work. *Amen.*

—Eleanor Lee McGee

Response to Psalm 84

How dear to me is your dwelling,
  O Lord of hosts!
My soul has a desire and longing for
  the courts of the Lord.

Oh Lord of hosts,
if I come to your banquet,
what shall I bring?
I shall not come empty-handed

but with pettiness simmering in
    my heart.
I shall come with a judging eye
scrutinizing your table.
I shall come with envy ladled out
over my wanting.
My spices are but tension,
ground to bits.

What I would bring to your banquet
should not be placed upon your
    table
but should be tied into bundles
and set afire
to become but ashes,
a reminder of my sin
burnt upon my heart. *Amen.*

—Evelina Moulder

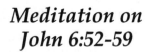

Meditation on John 6:52-59

He who eats my flesh and drinks my blood abides in me, and I in him.

(John 6:56)

Beckoning crystal, upheld
Light-filled goblet of scarlet,

> *The blood of our Lord Jesus*
> *Christ which was shed*
> *for thee*

droplets sparkling, glimmering
shimmering signs of wonder . . .
From my lips precious droplets
spill into my heart
and there create an abiding place
    for Christ
that I may make my dwelling
    place
deep within his mercy

And then I shall bring to your
    banquet
my heart
kindled anew with desire for you.
                       Amen.

             —Evelina Moulder

Sandalphon
(War: 16 January 1991)

In a dream
I see three angels
gathering prayers.
There is a legend
calling them by name;
these angels are the same.
And prayers, once prayed,
find their way, spinning,
drifting, spiraling toward the loom
in the angels' weaving room.

Here crowns are woven
all alike in beauty and design
and in the dream, the angel nods;
I may look for mine.

Joy, delight, deep and solemn
        praise,
psalms of every land
keep a patient rhythm
waiting an angel's hand.
And pressing on, my feet are
        soaked with tears.
I catch the poignant scent
of crushed and bruising fears.

From every prayer an angel
sweeps away a tarnished part—
an unkind thought, a selfish heart.
And children's prayers
are sweet melodious sounds
stitching together numberless
        woven crowns.

I hold the dream as closely
as I can;

it holds me while I come
into the light.
I kneel beside the window
upon waking
and understand
my crown is in the making. *Amen.*

—Beatrice W. Sims
(with permission[2])

The Watch

I watched for Christmas.
When it came,
it entered by another name.

The stars and moon
like shepherds led
my grateful self
to Jesus' bed.

The morning sun
appeared as planned.

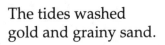

The tides washed
gold and grainy sand.

Who knows if oxen
munched the hay
next to the stall
where God's son lay?

Can anyone declare it true
the Virgin's colors
are white and blue?

We cling to old familiar carols.
We trim the tree.
We lose our place.
While all the time, our hectic search
is looking for the Christ Child's face.

Dear Jesus, we to Thee do bow when
we have wrung our spirits dry.
It took the cross
for us to know
the cradled Christ
could love us so! *Amen.*

—Beatrice W. Sims
(with permission[3])

Forgiveness

Have mercy on me and grant me a
  heart contrite and humble.

Merciful God, you give us so
  many possibilities of
  responding to you.
You give us beauty in creation.
You offer opportunities for joy.
Forgive moments lost in self-
  absorption.
Forgive opportunities lost and
  overlooked
To know you and make you
  known.
Through your generous and
  never-failing mercy,
Renew us.
Reawaken us.
Lead us through this life to eternal
  life.

Amen.

—Rosemari G. Sullivan

Prayer for an Awakened Heart

God of compassion and knowledge,
your constant love for each of us
excludes no one. Open my heart
today to all who will seek help
and counsel. Make me aware of
my own needs in the richness of
the truly poor and troublesome.
Never let me forget that in the
mystery of your presence you
are in each and every person I
encounter. Grant me a reverence
for all and a heart ever mindful
of your presence through the
grace of your Holy Spirit. *Amen.*

—Rosemari G. Sullivan

Twilight

The Buddhist comes mindful of
    his thought.
Female and Christian born, I come
    a paramour.
Love me, Lord, and above all else,
Grant this final grace to me:
Make my prayers more than
    thought,
Our time together more than my
    intention. *Amen.*

—Phyllis Tickle

Prayer Written at My Desk

Carpe diem?
It would be enough—
a sufficiency reaching glut—
simply to carpe momentum.

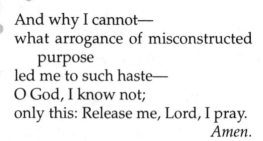

And why I cannot—
what arrogance of misconstructed
    purpose
led me to such haste—
O God, I know not;
only this: Release me, Lord, I pray.
                    Amen.

         —Phyllis Tickle

Beautiful Swimmer

If I had been able to cajole God
into manipulating life's events, my
children's lives would have turned
out differently.

On two separate occasions, within
one year, our daughter gave birth
to two sons, prematurely. After
carrying them swimming and
kicking in the womb for five
months, they were born too early

to survive. The best doctors, the best medicine, the best prayers could not bring the infants home in their parents' arms.

As I watch my daughter and her husband struggle with pain and loss, I see a different kind of love growing and bonding them. Changed forever by this experience, their knowledge of life's precious fragility adds new depth to their love. Born from grief, love takes on new dimensions, as God touches us in profound, dark hours.

Prayers change. I no longer present a list of what God should do to make our lives pain-free. Gone are the white picket fences and rose gardens of youthful dreams. In their place grows God's garden of the soul. Deep-rooted plants, filled with serendipity, sun,

rain and earth-smells testify to what
we can really depend on: God is
with us in all of life. We are loved.

For Ryan Alexander

Oh beautiful swimmer in the
    watery womb,
Apple of your father's eye,
Lovingly held, but for a moment,
    in your mother's arms,
Spirit-child born from love,
Touched to the earth lightly.
Sadly, we give you back to God.

—Barbara Townsend

Heartaches

Holy and gracious God,
our hearts ache at the loss of youth
    in our world.

Help us to heal.

Holy and gracious God,
our hearts ache as we watch our
loved ones die from disease.

> *Help us to mourn.*

Holy and gracious God,
our hearts ache from empty wombs.

> *Help us to love all children.*

Holy and gracious God,
our hearts ache from broken
   marriages.

> *Help us to find ways to*
> *mend relationships.*

Holy and gracious God,
our hearts ache from the divisions
   in our own church.

> *Help us to accept our*
> *differences.*

Holy and gracious God,
grow our hearts to find ways to fill
   the space you have provided.

*Space to love again, to forgive
those who offend, to accept
those who are different, to
demand the best of ourselves
and our partners, to learn
more about you.* Amen.

—Peggy Tuttle

Light

You bring us the light,
And you bring us the shadows.
Help us to know your presence in
    all things.
So that what the light illumines we
    shall see,
And what the shadows hide we
    shall not fear nor flee. *Amen.*

—Roberta Walmsley

Gloria

May the blessing of the Holy and
    Undivided Trinity;
God, who is three in One and
    One in Three;
Who is beyond us, among us,
    within us;
Who was and is and is to come,
    world without end,
Rest upon you and remain with you
    always. *Amen.*

—Catherine Waynick

Saturday

I gave myself a quiet day. I've never done this before. It was the first warm day of spring. There was no agenda but to ask God for images and guidance about two confusing relationships. At the end of the day I had a deep empathy and even deeper insight into my confusions. I felt love for someone I have never been able to love. The words, "Dear Lord and Father of Mankind" came to me. *Let us, like them, without a word, rise up and follow thee.* How blessed I am that the teachings of Jesus lead me to *rise up* to follow. Thanks be to God.
Amen.

—Betsy Wilson

Gracious God

We are your hands in the world.
Help us to care for those whom
    others have forgotten,
And to perform tasks that would
    otherwise go undone.
In times of fatigue and doubt,
Carry us in your heart of prayer;
In times of jubilation,
Enfold us with humility;
When misunderstood,
Give us the courage to press on.
When fallen in spirit,
Enfold us in the tender arms of
    your loving embrace. *Amen.*

—Geralyn Wolf

Biographical Information

Wendy Abrahamson, an art librarian from Saint Paul, Minnesota, is a postulant for Holy Orders, enrolled at the Virginia Theological Seminary.

The Rev. Dr. Vienna Cobb Anderson, educated and trained in the theater and the author of several books, is the former Rector of St. Margaret's Church, Washington, DC, and is currently Associate Rector, St. Paul's, Richmond, Virginia.

Margaret Graham Beers, an art historian, lives in Washington, DC, where she has raised five children and been active in St. Patrick's Church. She is involved with Forward Movement Publications as a member of the Executive Committee.

Avery Brooke, an oblate of the Episcopal monastic order of the Holy Cross, is a writer and spiritual director living in

Noroton, Connecticut. Her books include *Healing in the Landscape of Prayer*, *Finding God in the World*, *Plain Prayers in a Complicated World*.

Patricia Sparks Browning, originally from Corpus Christi, Texas, has spent the major portion of her adult life abroad doing missionary work while raising five children. She and her husband, the former Presiding Bishop, live in Oregon.

Sally Mitchell Bucklee has served the Episcopal Church in many capacities, most often as an advocate for the full participation of women in the church. Following a career in public health, she has been a consultant to a number of non-profit and religious organizations. She and her husband live in Maryland and have two children and three grandchildren.

Emily Blair Chewning is Writer-in-Residence at Wesley Theological Seminary in Washington, DC. She is the author of three books of non-fiction, and her work appears regularly in magazines and periodicals. The winner of an

American Book Award for *Anatomy Illustrated*, she is currently at work on a collection of poetry.

Pamela Pauley Chinnis is the President of the House of Deputies of the Episcopal Church and thereby its leading layperson. She lives in Washington, DC, and is the mother of two grown children.

Elizabeth Graham Cook, a recently retired business executive, is pursuing a graduate degree in Art Therapy. A native of New York, she has lived in Boston all of her adult life, where she is active in Trinity Church and with the Society of Saint John the Evangelist.

The Rev. Barbara Crafton is the Rector of St. Clement's Church in New York City and the author of *Blessed Paradoxes: The Beatitudes as Painted Prayer* and *The Sewing Room*, as well as numerous other works.

The Rev. Margaret M. Graham is the Rector of St. John's Church, Georgetown in Washington, DC. A Chicago native, she and her husband raised their children in Washington.

Phoebe W. Griswold sees herself as a catalyst of good works. Her current role as the wife of the Presiding Bishop gives her many opportunities to connect people and needs, and to see the joys of holy creativity.

The Rev. Margaret Brown Gunness, a graduate of the Episcopal Divinity School, is former Interim Rector of Christ Church, Cambridge, Massachusetts, former Rector of Christ Church, Ridgewood, New Jersey and is Vicar of Calvary Church, Memphis, Tennessee. She and her husband have three grown children and one grandchild.

Betty Vilas Hedblom is a Midwesterner living close to the shores of Lake Michigan. A child-welfare worker with a long-time interest in issues of social justice, she is a member of the Society of the Companions of the Holy Cross.

The Very Rev. Martha Johnston Horne is the Dean and President of Virginia Theological Seminary. A native of North Carolina, she and her husband have two grown children.

Anne Shelburne Jones, poet and teacher, has led retreats and conferences for the Episcopal Church, is the mother of three and grandmother of two. She lives in Indianapolis with her husband, the former Bishop of Indianapolis.

Mary Page de Bordenave Jones is a native of Virginia, rooted deep in the Episcopal Church, which she has served in multiple capacities for her entire life. She and her husband currently live in Jerusalem at St. George's College, where he is Dean.

The Rev. Eleanor Lee McGee is an Associate Professor of Pastoral Counseling, Yale Divinity School and the author of numerous scholarly articles. She was formerly Rector of St. Paul's, New Haven, has two grown sons, a guide dog and a horse.

Evelina Randolph Moulder, working poet, writer, and publisher for a non-profit association, is pursuing a Master's degree in Theological Studies at Virginia Theological Seminary and is a member of Immanuel Church-on-the-Hill, Alexandria.

Beatrice W. Sims is a poet presently living near a mountain lake in Central Pennsylvania. Born on the prairie of western Kansas, she has an eye for, and an ongoing conversation with, the natural environment. Closely involved with the work of the church through much of her adult life, she is a member of the Society of the Companions of the Holy Cross.

The Rev. Rosemari Gaughan Sullivan is the Executive Officer and Secretary of the General Convention of the Episcopal Church. She has served as Rector of The Church of St. Clement, Alexandria, Virginia, and is an Oblate of the Order of St. Benedict at the Mount St. Scholastic Monastery in Kansas. She and her husband have two grown children.

Phyllis Alexander Tickle, an active Episcopal laywoman and Eucharistic Minister, is Contributing Editor in Religion for *Publisher's Weekly*, and the author of *God-Talk in America*. She is also the compiler of *The Divine Hours*, a contemporary prayer manual. She and her husband have seven grown children.

Barbara Gunderman Townsend, a pilgrim to holy Celtic places, a penny-whistle player, an occasional retreat leader and writer, a builder in rock, enjoys garden spaces and her lovely grand-daughter. She makes her home on a farm on the Eastern Shore of Maryland, where her husband is the Bishop of the Diocese of Easton. They have three grown children.

The Rev. Peggy Elaine Tuttle is the Rector of the Church of the Advent in Farmington, Minnesota. A native of Fort Worth, Texas, she and her husband have lived and raised their family in Louisiana, Oklahoma, Washington, DC, and Colorado. She is a graduate of Virginia Theological Seminary.

Roberta Chapin Walmsley is the Companion-in-Charge of the Society of the Companions of the Holy Cross. A retired social worker, she is the co-author of *Healthy Clergy, Wounded Healers: Their Families and Their Ministries*. Mrs. Walmsley and her husband, the retired Bishop of Connecticut, have two grown children and live in New Hampshire, where she is active as an organist.

The Rt. Rev. Catherine Maples Waynick, a native of Mississippi, is the Bishop of the Diocese of Indianapolis, where she lives with her husband. They have two married children.

Elizabeth Reed Wilson is the Director of *Let's Face It USA*, a support network for people with facial disfigurement (www.faceit.org/letsfaceit). An early childhood educator, she lives in the Northwest near her children and grandchildren.

The Rt. Rev. Geralyn Wolf is the Episcopal Bishop of the Diocese of Rhode Island. A native of New York, she is an Associate of Gethsemane Abbey in Kentucky.

Notes

[1] Avery Brook, "Suburban Litany" from *The Wideness of God's Mercy*. Vol. I, Jeffrey Rowthorn, ed., Seabury Press, New York, 1985.

[2,3] Beatrice Sims, "Sandalphon" and "The Watch" from *Found Poems*, Rural Sophisticate Press, Maysville, GA, 1992.